CLOSE-UP

BACKYARD

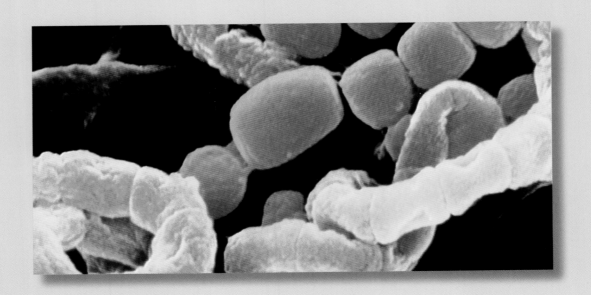

BROWN
BEAR
BOOKS

Published by Brown Bear Books Limited

An imprint of
The Brown Reference Group plc
68 Topstone Road
Redding
Connecticut
06896
USA
www.brownreference.com

ISBN: 978-1-93383-413-9

Authors: John Woodward and Leon Gray
Designer: Lynne Lennon
Picture Researcher: Rupert Palmer
Managing Editor: Bridget Giles
Production Director: Alastair Gourlay
Children's Publisher: Anne O'Daly

Picture credits
Front cover: Science Photo Library; David Scharf
Title page: Science Photo Library; Dr. Jeremy Burgess
Science Photo Library: James Bell 13; Dr. Jeremy Burgess 5, 9, 15, 21;
Eye of Science 19, 29; David Scharf 17, 23; Andrew Syred 7, 25, 27;
Dr. Keith Wheeler 11.

Library of Congress Cataloging-in-Publication Data

Backyard.

    p. cm. – (Close-up)

Includes index.

ISBN-13: 978-1-933834-13-9 (alk. paper)

1. Nature study–Juvenile literature. 2. Natural history–Juvenile literature.

QH51 .B13 2007

508 22 dc.22

2006103049

Printed in China
9 8 7 6 5 4 3 2 1

Contents

Helpful Bacteria

Tiny creatures called bacteria live in the soil in your backyard. Bacteria eat dead animals and plants. As they eat, the bacteria put important chemicals back into the soil. These chemicals help new plants grow. Animals then feed on the new plants.

Good and bad

Sometimes bad bacteria grow inside our bodies and make us feel ill. Most bacteria are harmless. We need them for life. All the animals and plants on Earth would die if there were no bacteria.

Tiny Pioneers

Bacteria were probably the first living things to appear on Earth, millions of years ago. They have changed very little since then. Bacteria are very small. Thousands of bacteria would fit on the period at the end of this sentence.

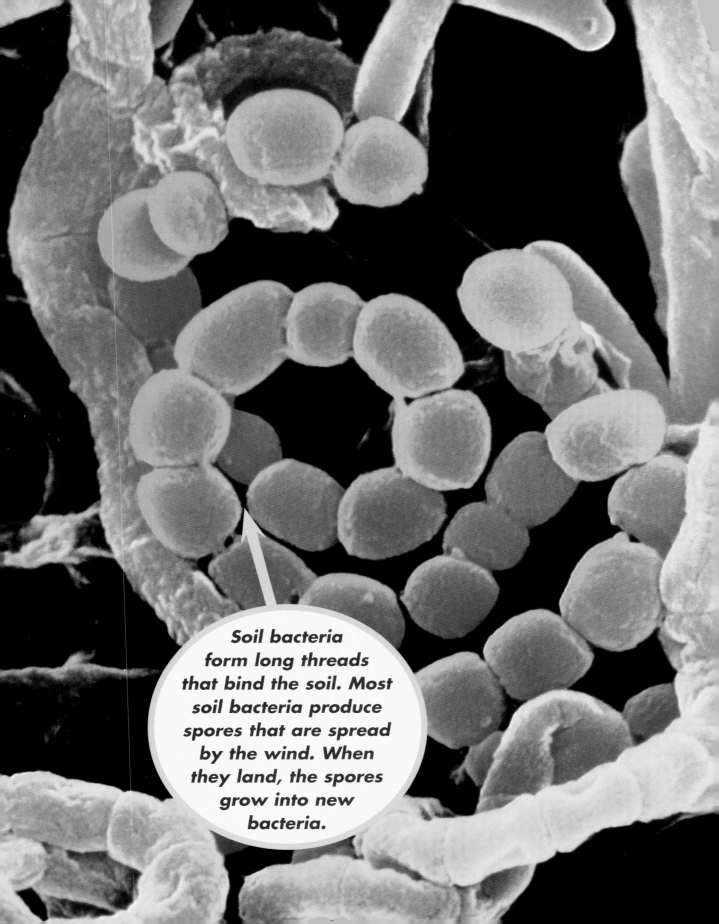

Soil bacteria form long threads that bind the soil. Most soil bacteria produce spores that are spread by the wind. When they land, the spores grow into new bacteria.

Algae Alert

In summer, tiny plantlike creatures called algae form a slime on the surfaces of ponds. The slime is usually green. Some algae turn a pond red. Algae are made of single cells. The cells of some algae join up in long chains. More algae grow in the summer because the water is warmer.

Giant Algae

Algae are usually too small to see with the eyes alone. Scientists use microscopes to study them. Other algae are large plants. Kelp are giant algae that live in underwater "forests" in the sea. Kelp forests grow off the coast of California. The seaweed we find on beaches are also giant algae.

Pond pollution

When algae die, they rot away and pollute the pond water. The rotting algae use up a gas called oxygen in the water. Fish and other pond animals need oxygen to breathe. Most pond animals die if there is rotting algae in the water.

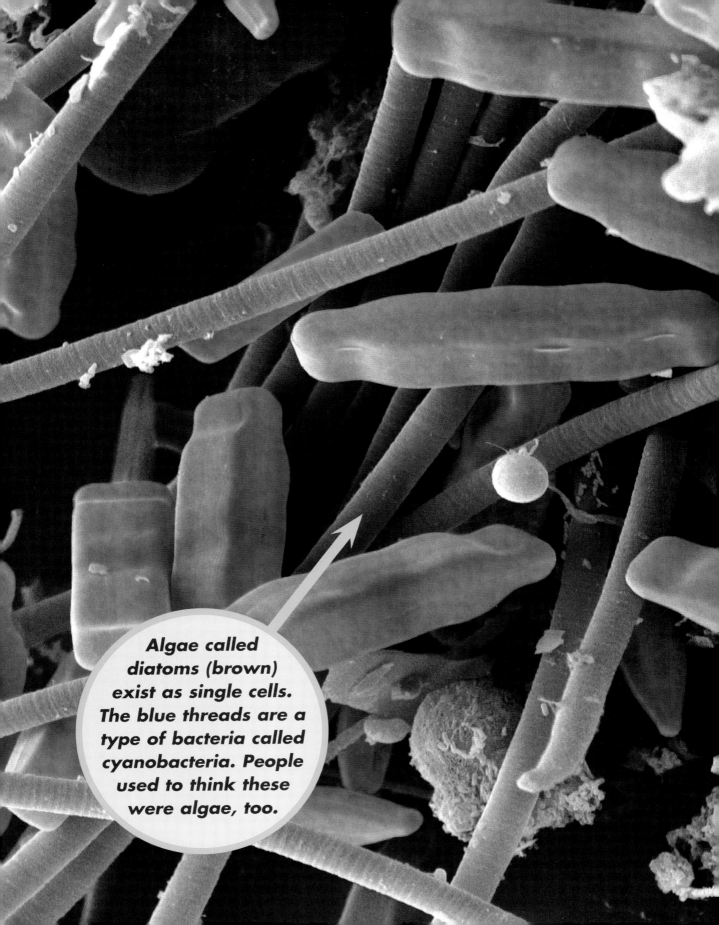

Algae called diatoms (brown) exist as single cells. The blue threads are a type of bacteria called cyanobacteria. People used to think these were algae, too.

Made in the Shade

Ferns are plants that do not have colorful flowers. They look like small trees. Ferns do not grow from seeds like most plants. Instead, they produce tiny spores that blow in the wind. If the spore lands in a dark, damp place, it may grow into a new fern.

Water lovers

Ferns grow best where there is plenty of water. Many ferns grow in tropical forests, where it is hot and there is lots of rain. Other ferns float in water. These floating ferns can cover an entire lake.

Fern Forests

Millions of years ago, there were no plants with flowers. Instead, great fern forests covered the land. When the ferns died, their remains became buried in the soil. The weight of the soil pushed down on the dead plants. Over millions of years, the dead ferns turned into coal.

These orange balls are sori. They stick to the underside of the fern's leaves. The sori hold the spores that will grow into new fern plants.

Life Force

Most plants need a regular supply of water to grow and stay healthy. The roots of a plant draw water from the soil. Tubes in the plant's stem carry this water up from the roots. The plant makes food in its leaves using energy from the Sun. Tubes in the plant's stem carry the food to where it is needed.

Water Pressure

Try this experiment to see how important water is to a plant. Ask an adult to help you cut a plant at the base of its stem. Put the cut plant in an empty jar. Leave the plant in the Sun. In the heat, the plant loses water and droops. Pour some water into the jar. Watch as the plant becomes stiff again.

Losing water

If the Sun is too hot, the plant can lose water from the leaves. The roots will try to draw more water from the soil. If there is no water, the plant's leaves and stem will droop. The plant may die if it does not get water quickly.

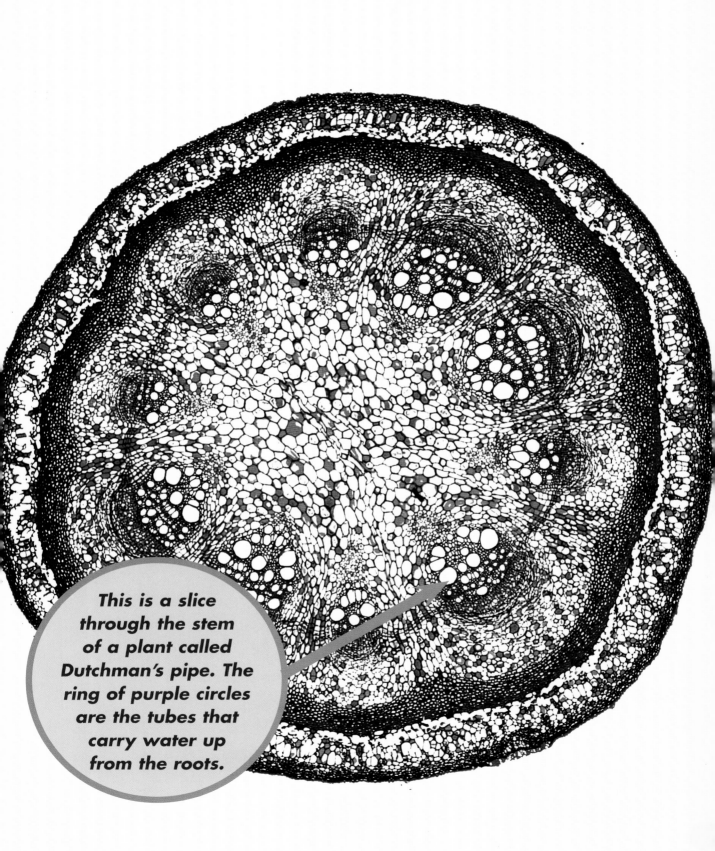

High Fiber

Plants are made up of millions and millions of tiny cells. Cells are the building blocks of all living things. Plant cells are surrounded by a tough wall of cellulose. Cellulose is a type of sugar. It forms strong fibers that keep the plant firm but springy.

Tall trees

The cells in a tree are very strong. The cellulose in the cell wall mixes with a substance called lignin. The mixture is called wood. Wood helps trees grow much taller than other plants.

Record Breakers

Some trees are amazingly tall. In Australia, trees called mountain ashes grow up to 390 feet (120 meters) tall. That's higher than a 30-story building. The giant sequoias of California are the tallest trees in the United States. They grow up to 300 feet (90 meters) tall.

Air to Spare

Plants need gases called oxygen and carbon dioxide to breathe. They get these gases from the air. Some plants live underwater. How do they get air? Small water plants usually get oxygen and carbon dioxide from gases dissolved in the water. Larger plants must find other ways of getting the air they need.

Swamp Snorkels

Some swamp plants have unusual ways to get air to their roots. Trees called swamp cypresses live in places where there is lots of mud and water. The trees have woody spikes that grow up from roots in the mud. The spikes are spongy tubes with small holes that open into the air.

Underwater air

Plants called water lilies have special leaves that are filled with air spaces. The air makes the leaves float on the surface of the water. The leaves draw in air. The air passes through tubes down to the underwater roots.

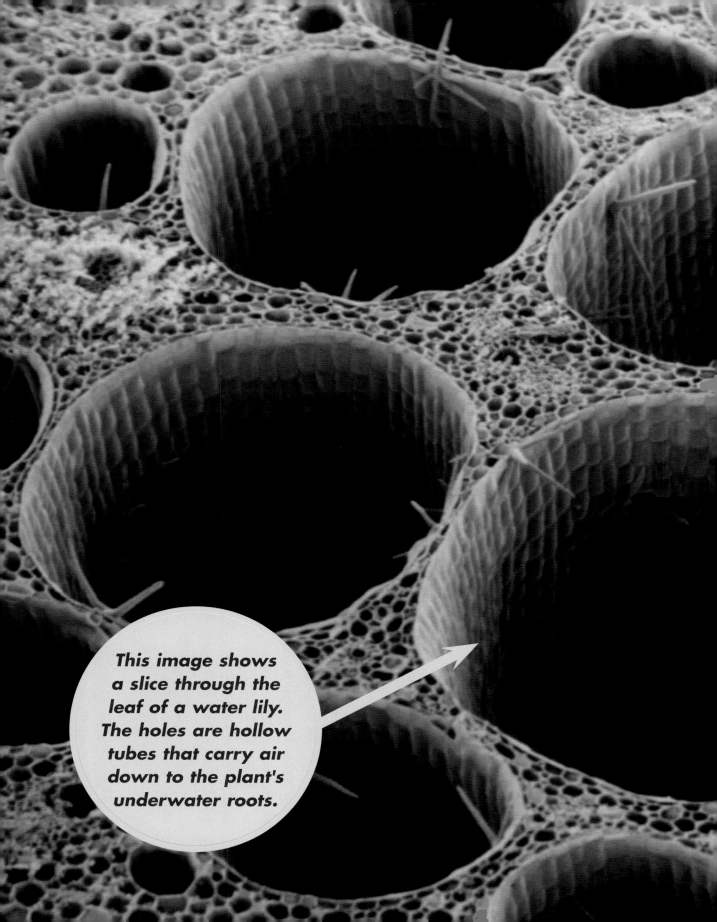

Mighty Mites

If you look in the grass in your backyard you will probably find a mite. These tiny animals look like spiders. They have eight legs and hairy bodies. Most mites eat other tiny animals or scraps of food they find in the grass.

Bloodsucking mites

Some mites bite through our skin and suck blood from our bodies. The bite may cause an itchy rash that lasts for days. Some mites cause a deadly illness called scrub-typhus, but this is very rare.

Lying in Wait

People pick up bloodsucking mites when they walk through thick grass. Mites can smell a gas called carbon dioxide in the air people breathe out. The mites home in on the carbon dioxide and jump up onto the body. They are so small that they can pass through clothes to get to the skin.

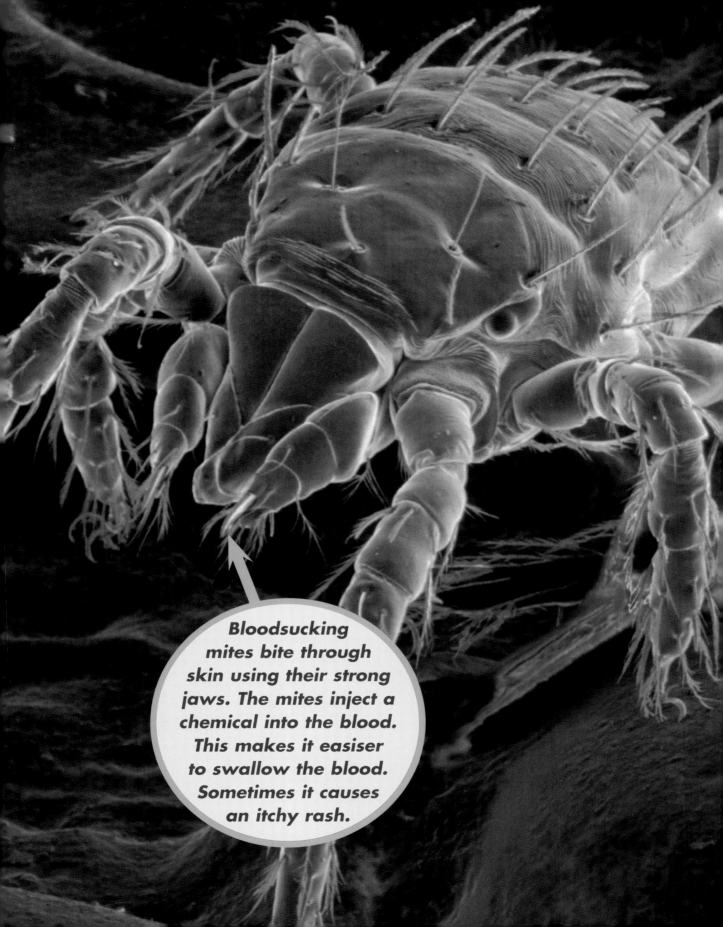

Bloodsucking mites bite through skin using their strong jaws. The mites inject a chemical into the blood. This makes it easiser to swallow the blood. Sometimes it causes an itchy rash.

At the Root

When a seed starts to grow it splits open. The first thing to appear is the root. The root grows down into the soil. Fine hairs grow out from the tip of the root. The root hairs spread out in the soil and soak up any water. The plant will also soak up food in the water, which helps the plant grow.

Sow and Grow

Try an experiment to grow a plant from its seed. First put a few seeds on a piece of wet tissue paper. Leave the paper and seeds in a warm place. The roots will appear within a few days. Keep the tissue paper moist. The roots will grow longer. The first green leaves will also start to grow.

Root cap

The root tip is covered with a tough cap. This cap allows the root to grow between hard objects in the soil without damaging the root. Roots can even push through the cracks in hard concrete in their search for water.

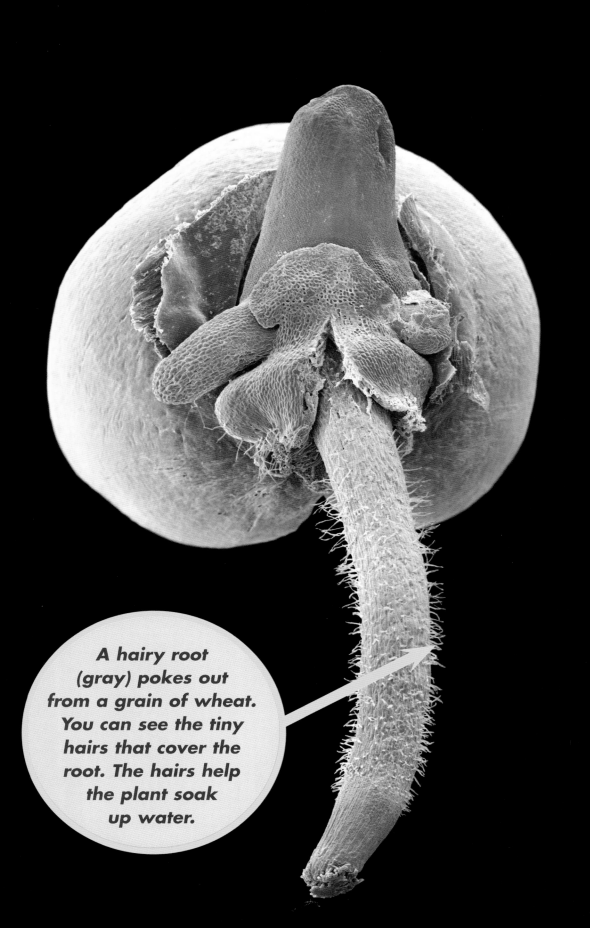

A hairy root (gray) pokes out from a grain of wheat. You can see the tiny hairs that cover the root. The hairs help the plant soak up water.

From Death into Life

When an animal or plant dies, it rots in the soil. Millions of tiny animals feed on the dead body. The dead animal or plant becomes food for living plants. In turn, the plants are food for living animals.

Soil animals

Mites and nematodes live in the soil. Mites look like small spiders. They have eight legs, hairy bodies, and a strong bite. Nematodes are tiny worms with smooth bodies.

Worms Crawl In

Some of the tiny animals that live in the soil are harmful. Some soil nematodes spend part of their lives inside the bodies of living animals, including people. They feed on the body and make people ill.

A mite and a nematode meet in the soil. Mites and nematodes break up the bodies of dead animals and plants. This makes food for living plants.

Earth Movers

Earthworms dig tunnels in the soil. As they dig, they swallow soil and eat the scraps of food that they find. Earthworms are very good for the soil in your backyard. Their tunnels let air into the ground. They help water drain through the soil.

Sinking Stones

The soil that passes through an earthworm is smooth and free of stones. Earthworms can swallow soft soil. Hard stones cannot pass through their bodies. If an earthworm bumps into a stone it will dig under it. The stone then sinks into the soil. Plants find it easier to grow in soil where there are fewer stones.

Plant pals

Earthworms help plants grow in the soil. As an earthworm feeds, the soil that it eats passes through its body. The earthworm gets rid of waste soil at the surface of the ground. The waste soil is rich in foods that plants eat. Many plants cannot grow in places where there are no earthworms in the soil.

22

An earthworm head on. The worm has no eyes. It is strong enough to push through hard soil. The worm senses light and always digs away from it.

Toothful Wonders

Have you ever seen thin, silvery trails in your backyard? These trails are left by slugs and snails. Slugs and snails move by sliding over a film of slime. The slime covers their "foot." A slug's foot moves in waves. The waves push the slug along the ground.

Tongue teeth

Slugs and snails eat plants. They scrape their tongues over the plants. The tongues are covered with hard "teeth." The teeth form at the back of the tongue. New teeth push forward to replace the worn teeth.

Snail Slime

Put a snail on a piece of glass. When the snail starts to move, ask an adult to turn the glass upside down. Look at the waves passing down the foot as the snail slides over the film of slime. When you have finished, put the snail back where you found it.

Spider Soup

Many different spiders live in the dark corners of your backyard. All spiders have eight legs, a hairy body, and long fangs. Some spiders build webs from silk. The web traps tiny animals. The spider bites the animal with its fangs. Poison in the spider's bite stops the animal from moving.

Strong Silk

A spider always builds its web in the same way. It follows the same order from start to finish. The spider makes the silk in sacs called glands. The silk leaves the body through holes called spinnerets. Spider silk is strong. A strand of silk is much stronger than a matching strand of steel.

Spider soup

When the animal is still, the spider ties up its victim with silk. A spider cannot swallow solid food. It uses chemicals to turn the insides of the animal into a liquid "soup." The spider then sucks out its liquid meal. All that it leaves behind is an empty shell.

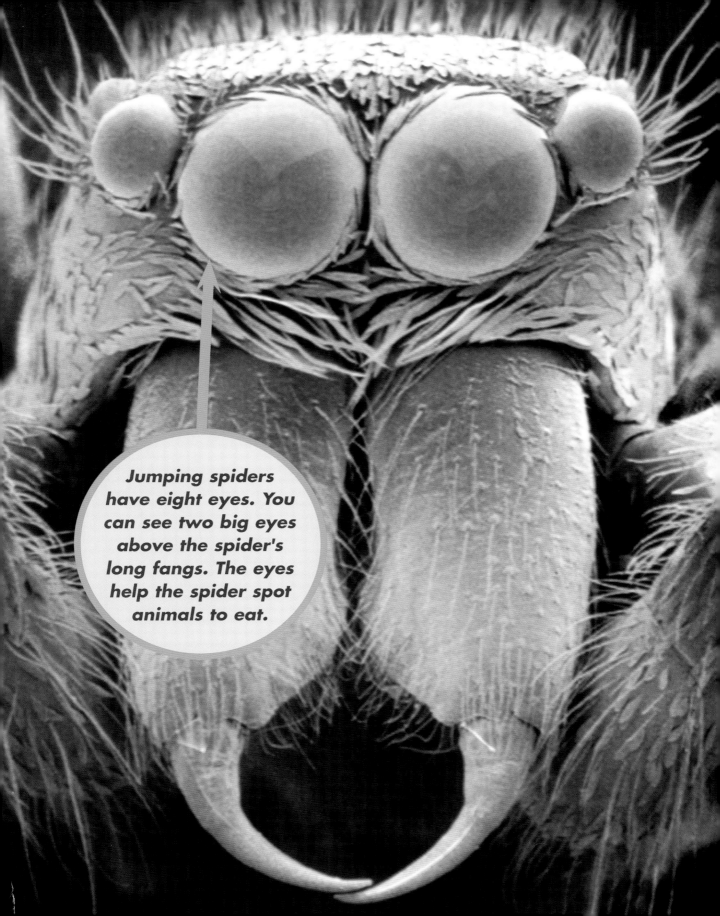

Rusting Away

Many people leave metal trash in their backyard. Some of it will be rusty. Rust happens when a metal called iron gets wet. Water makes the iron mix with a gas called oxygen in the air. The iron and oxygen turn into a chemical called iron oxide. That is rust.

Rust rot

Anything made from iron will rust. An old car will have rust on it. Small patches of rust are easy to clean. If the rust is left for a long time, the metal will start to rot. In the end, it will rust away to nothing.

Rustproofing

The best way to stop rust from forming is to coat the iron. A coat of paint stops water and oxygen from attacking the iron. Metals such as tin are also used to coat iron to stop it from rusting.

Glossary

algae: plantlike creatures made up of single cells.

bacteria: tiny, single-celled creatures that can be helpful or harmful to people.

cells: tiny building blocks that make up the bodies of all living creatures.

cellulose: the tough substance that makes up the cell walls of plants.

chemical: any substance found in nature or made by people.

lignin: the substance that mixes with cellulose to make wood.

poison: a substance that harms living creatures.

pollute: damage the air, soil, or water by adding harmful substances.

roots: parts of a plant that draw up water from soil.

rust: the brown substance that builds up on metals after they get wet.

seed: the part of a plant that grows in the soil and becomes a new plant.

sori: tiny balls that grow on a fern's leaves and contain the fern's spores.

spore: the tiny "seed" of a fern or fungus that grows in the soil and becomes a new fern or fungus.

stem: the part of a plant bearing leaves and flowers.

Further Study

Books

Bishop, Nic. *Backyard Detective: Critters Up Close.* New York: Tangerine Press, 2002.

Hewitt, Sally. *Your Backyard (Discovering Nature).* East Grinstead, Sussex, UK: Copper Beech, 2000.

Levine, Shar, Johnstone, Leslie, and Garbot, Dave. *Backyard Science.* New York: Sterling, 2005.

Macaulay, Kelley, and Bobbie Kalman. *Backyard Habitats (Introducing Habitats).* New York: Crabtree Publishing Company, 2006.

Ross, Michael Elsohn, Grogan, Brian, and Erickson, Darren. *Snailology (Backyard Buddies).* Minnaepolis: Carolrhoda Books, 1996.

Web sites

youtube.com/group/BackyardCreatures
Watch videos of living creatures found in the backyard and neighborhood park on this popular community web site.

www.backyardnature.net
Learn about all the animals and plants living in your backyard using this online nature study guide.

Index